Dear Supporters,

Welcome to the Official Tottenham Hotspur Annual 2020.

What a year 2019 was for Spurs as the Club celebrated the opening of our new stadium and embarked on an incredible journey to the UEFA Champions League Final in Madrid. In the Premier League, we managed another top four finish to achieve qualification for the Champions League for a fourth consecutive year while we also reached the semi-final of the Carabao Cup.

In this Annual, we'll take a look back on an unforgettable 2018/19 season, which saw us beat the likes of Arsenal, Ajax, Borussia Dortmund, Chelsea, Inter Milan, Manchester City and Manchester United in various competitions. We profile our new signings, explore our new stadium, while there are also quizzes, games, posters and plenty more besides.

Enjoy your new Annual and COME ON YOU SPURS!

#COYS

Contents

THE ROAD TO MADRID

Our UEFA Champions League campaign of 2018/19 was a rollercoaster ride that eventually saw us progress to the final of the competition. Editor Andy Greeves reflects on a spectacular journey that will live long in the memory.

GROUP B

MATCHDAY ONE
Internazionale 2-1 Spurs

In our opening Group B fixture, Christian Eriksen gave us a second-half lead with a looping shot over Inter goalkeeper Samir Handanovic. With only five minutes of the match remaining, Argentinian international Mauro Icardi equalised for the Nerazzurri with a 20-yard volley. Hopes of returning from San Siro with a credible point were dashed in the second minute of injury time when Uruguayan midfielder Matias Vecino rose above our defence to head Inter's winner.

MATCHDAY TWO
Spurs 2-4 Barcelona

A crowd of 82,137 packed into Wembley Stadium for our eagerly anticipated clash with Spanish giants Barcelona. Philippe Coutinho put Barca ahead after just two minutes and Ivan Rakitic doubled the visitors' advantage with a spectacular 20-yard effort before the break. A spirited second-half showing from Mauricio Pochettino's side was rewarded when Harry Kane got a goal back. Lionel Messi restored the Catalans' two-goal advantage before compatriot Erik Lamela's 66th minute strike for us. An entertaining game was settled in the final minute of normal time when Messi slotted home after a clever dummy from Luis Suarez.

MATCHDAY THREE
PSV Eindhoven 2-2 Spurs

Mauricio admitted our chances of reaching the Champions League knockout stages were "nearly over" after we were unable to secure a victory against Dutch side PSV Eindhoven. Mexican international Hirving Lozano capitalised on a defensive error to put the hosts one up on the half-hour mark. Lucas Moura levelled before the break prior to Kane's goal 10 minutes into the second-half that put us in the ascendancy. Skipper Hugo Lloris was sent off with 11 minutes of the game remaining and PSV made their one-man advantage pay, with Luuk de Jong equalising late on.

MATCHDAY FOUR
Spurs 2-1 PSV Eindhoven

In relation to our hopes of making it through the knockout phase, our home game with PSV Eindhoven was a 'must-win' occasion having accrued just one point from our opening three group fixtures. After de Jong gave PSV an early lead, our players responded with a battling performance to claim a 2-1 victory. Kane levelled on 78 minutes with a firmly struck, left-footed shot. He then grabbed the winner with a minute of normal time remaining, his header from a Ben Davies cross deflecting off defender Trent Sainsbury and beating Jeroen Zoet in the Eindhoven goal.

MATCHDAY FIVE
Spurs 1-0 Internazionale

We left it late to claim another vital Champions League victory at Wembley Stadium. Eriksen, who replaced Lamela as a 70th minute substitute, got the only goal of the game with 10 minutes left on the clock. The Dane got on the end of a fine pass from Dele before firing home with his left foot.

MATCHDAY SIX
Barcelona 1-1 Spurs

We travelled to the Nou Camp knowing we needed to match or better Inter's result at home to PSV Eindhoven in the final group stage matches to make it through to the knockout phase. Ousmane Dembele scored after just seven minutes of the match for Barcelona, as we briefly dropped out of second position in the Group B table. Lozano's goal for PSV at San Siro moments later put us back in the ascendancy but Icardi's second-half equaliser for Inter left us needing at least one goal in Spain. Lucas came up with our all-important leveller five minutes from time and with both ourselves and PSV holding on for 1-1 draws, we progressed to the round of 16 by virtue of a better head-to-head record against Inter.

GROUP B TABLE

		P	W	D	L	GF	GA	GD	PTS
1	Barcelona	6	4	2	0	14	5	+9	14
2	Spurs	6	2	2	2	9	10	−1	8
3	Inter Milan	6	2	2	2	6	7	−1	8
4	PSV Eindhoven	6	0	2	4	6	13	−7	2

KNOCKOUT PHASE

ROUND OF 16, FIRST LEG
Spurs 3-0 Borussia Dortmund

Having faced Borussia Dortmund in two of the previous three seasons in both the UEFA Europa League and the Champions League, the German side were familiar opponents. After a goalless first-half, a memorable display in the second period saw us run out 3-0 winners in our last 'home' European tie at Wembley Stadium. Heung-Min Son put us in front with a controlled volley from a Jan Vertonghen cross two minutes after the break. Vertonghen showed similar composure to get our second goal seven minutes from time while Fernando Llorente increased our advantage moments later.

ROUND OF 16, SECOND LEG
Borussia Dortmund 0-1 Spurs
(Spurs win 4-0 on aggregate)

We survived an early siege on our goal to ensure an ultimately comfortable passage through to the quarter final phase at Dortmund's Westfalenstadion. A mixture of fine defensive work and several excellent saves from Hugo Lloris meant we kept a clean sheet in both home and away matches against the German giants. At the other end, Harry Kane's assured finish four minutes after the break sealed a 4-0 aggregate win.

QUARTER-FINAL

FIRST LEG
Spurs 1-0 Manchester City

Hugo Lloris' first-half penalty save from Sergio Aguero proved to be a massive moment in the context of our all-English quarter-final tie against Manchester City. With 12 minutes remaining in our first-ever European match at the Tottenham Hotspur Stadium, Son twisted and turned through the Citizens' defence before firing low past goalkeeper Ederson to give us a first-leg lead.

SECOND LEG
Manchester City 4-3 Spurs
(4-4 on aggregate – Spurs win on away goals)

Five goals in the opening 21 minutes at the Etihad Stadium lit the touch paper on a night of high drama in Manchester. Raheem Sterling made it 1-1 on aggregate after just three minutes and 51 seconds before a quick brace from Son put us 2-1 up on the night and 3-1 overall. Bernado Silva and a second strike from Sterling followed as the players left the field with the score level at 3-3 on aggregate at the break. Aguero gave City the overall lead for the first time 14 minutes into the second-half but substitute Llorente drew us level 13 minutes from time. Our hopes of making it to the semi-finals looked to have been cruelly dashed when Sterling scored again in stoppage time at the end of the match. However, the Video Assistant Referee (VAR) revealed that Aguero had been in an offside position during the move and Sterling's 'goal' was disallowed. The 4-4 draw was enough to put us through to the last four on the away goals rule.

FIRST LEG
Spurs 0-1 Ajax

After the drama of the Etihad, our semi-final, first leg match against Ajax was a more sedate affair. Donny van de Beek finished a slick passing move to put the Dutch club one-up after 15 minutes of the match. Headers from Llorente and Toby Alderweireld, that went narrowly wide, were the closest we came to an equaliser on a disappointing night in N17.

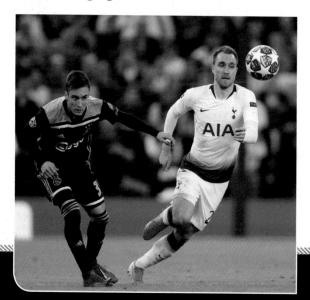

SECOND LEG

Ajax 2-3 Spurs
(3-3 on aggregate – Spurs win on away goals)

Not for the first time in the season, we stared elimination from the Champions League in the face as we trailed 2-0 at half-time – and 3-0 on aggregate – in our semi-final, second leg match in Amsterdam. Goals from Matthijs de Ligt and Hakim Ziyech looked to have put the tie beyond us at the Johan Cruyff Arena. The night before, Liverpool overturned a 3-0 first leg defeat to beat Barcelona 4-3 on aggregate. Our players produced an equally spectacular turnaround in the second-half in the Netherlands. Two goals from Lucas before the hour mark brought us back into the tie prior to the most incredible end to the match. In the sixth minute of injury time, Moussa Sissoko's long-ball was touched on by substitute Llorente. Moura ran onto Dele's deft pass inside the penalty area before placing a low shot beyond the reach of Ajax goalkeeper Andre Onana. "They've done it… I cannot believe it," screamed BT Sport commentator Darren Fletcher as our players and fans celebrated the Brazilian's hat-trick goal and a monumental moment in our history.

FINAL

Spurs 0-2 Liverpool

Atletico Madrid's Estadio Metropolitano was the setting for our first-ever Champions League Final. Liverpool – who had won the European Cup on five previous occasions – were awarded a penalty in the opening minute of the match when Sissoko was adjudged to have handled a cross from Sadio Mane. Mohamed Salah dispatched the resulting spot-kick beyond the dive of Spurs captain Hugo Lloris. With three minutes of the match remaining, substitute Divock Origi sealed the Reds' victory with a low drive from inside our penalty area, bringing to an end our dramatic and emotional Champions League campaign.

HOME SWEET HOME

Opened in 2019, Tottenham Hotspur Stadium is our brand-new, state-of-the-art home.

The date 3 April 2019 was a special one in the history of Tottenham Hotspur Football Club as we staged our inaugural First Team match at the Tottenham Hotspur Stadium.

Before the Premier League game against Crystal Palace, the stadium's opening ceremony took place, which featured video content and musical performances from the likes of X Factor star Lanya Matthews, world-renowned tenor Wynne Evans, children from Gladesmore

Community School and the Tottenham Hotspur Marching Band. There was also a spectacular firework display prior to kick-off.

Heung-Min Son scored the first senior goal at the ground with a 55th minute strike against the Eagles, while Christian Eriksen was also on target in a 2-0 victory on a night no Spurs supporter will ever forget.

A series of test events took place at the ground prior to its full opening, which included an Under-18 Premier League clash against Southampton on 24 March 2019. J'Neil Bennett scored the first-ever goal at the Tottenham Hotspur Stadium after 11 minutes of that clash, watched by almost 30,000. Harvey White (penalty) and Dilan Markanday were also on target for our academy side that afternoon, while Kornelius Hansen got a consolation for Saints.

Six days later, club greats such as Jurgen Klinsmann, David Ginola and Paul Gascoigne lined up at our new home for the 'Spurs Legends' team in a thrilling match against 'Inter Forever'. Full details of the exhibition game can be found on pages 58 and 59 of this annual.

Designed by Populous, the Tottenham Hotspur Stadium has a host of unique features including the world's first dividing retractable pitch, enabling us to stage NFL fixtures, concerts and other sporting events in addition to football matches.

> **Situated behind one of the goals is the South Stand, which is the largest single-tier stand in the UK, holding 17,500 fans on a matchday, to create a 'wall of sound'.**

The supporter experience at the new stadium is second-to-none with modern seating, generous leg room and uninterrupted views of the pitch not to mention over 60 food and drink outlets. The angle of the four stands has been set at 35 degrees and this, combined with supporters' close proximity to the pitch, optimises the atmosphere created on a matchday. Situated behind one of the goals is the South Stand, which is the largest single-tier stand in the UK, holding 17,500 fans on a matchday, to create a 'wall of sound'.

The players' changing rooms, tunnel, dugouts and Directors' Box can be found in the West Stand, while the NFL locker rooms are over in the East Stand. The North Stand meanwhile has a designated Family Area as well as accommodating visiting supporters. The concourse flooring throughout the ground contains crushed aggregate from the foundations of our former White Hart Lane home, meaning supporters have history beneath their feet as they make their way around our new stadium.

There are other nods to our past throughout the stadium. A plaque can be found within the South Atrium that marks the position of the centre spot from our former home White Hart Lane, while a display of iconic programme covers is located in the south-west corner of the ground. Names of all our Official Supporters' Clubs can be found on North East Level 1 concourse

while there is an art gallery on the West Level 1 concourse showcasing the work of local artists including Albert 'Agwa' Clegg, Ashton Attzs, Marina Nimmo and Natsko Seki.

Four large HD screens – the largest in the UK – are situated in the four corners of the stadium offering match action, replays and pre-match/half-time entertainment while 1,800 HD TVs can be found elsewhere in the ground. There's also free WiFi and high-density mobile connectivity, giving supporters the perfect opportunity to engage with the club on its various social media platforms!

Outside the ground, the historic Warmington House – which was built back in 1828 – has been renovated and is now home to the 'Tottenham Experience' – which accommodates the Spurs Megastore – the largest football club shop in Europe – as well as the forthcoming Club Museum and Tottenham Hotspur Archive.

In addition to stadium tours, visitors will also be able to experience the spectacular Sky Walk – an adrenaline-filled attraction where you scale the Tottenham Hotspur Stadium and step on the glass walkway 40 metres above the pitch.

No Spurs supporter will forget their first visit to the Tottenham Hotspur Stadium which Club chairman Daniel Levy describes as "our new home for generations".

SEASON REVIEW
2018/19

The 2018/19 season saw Spurs finish fourth in the Premier League – the fourth consecutive campaign we have claimed a top four spot and qualified for UEFA Champions League football. It was our best run of league finishes since Bill Nicholson's 'glory glory' side came fourth or above for five back-to-back campaigns in the old First Division between 1959/60 and 1963/64. We only drew two Premier League matches all season – a new Club record, while our 11 away victories in the division was our best return on the road since 1984/85, when we achieved 12 wins on our travels.

AUGUST

We made a perfect start to the 2018/19 season with three wins out of three in August.

First-half goals from Jan Vertonghen and Dele Alli gave us a 2-1 win at Newcastle United on the opening day of the campaign. A week later, we beat Fulham 3-1 at our temporary 'home', Wembley Stadium. Lucas Moura netted just before half-time while second-half strikes from Kieran Trippier and Harry Kane secured the points.

The month ended with a memorable 3-0 success away at Manchester United. Lucas bagged a brace while Kane grabbed his second goal in successive matches in the triumph.

A sixth-minute strike from Eric Dier was enough to give us a 1-0 home victory over Cardiff City in October. Our fourth consecutive league victory came at West Ham United a few weeks later as Lamela continued his excellent form in front of goal.

A battling display against would-be Premier League champions Manchester City was not enough to prevent the Citizens claiming a 1-0 triumph at Wembley.

SEPTEMBER

Despite leading through an Abdoulaye Doucoure own goal, we slumped to our first defeat of the campaign at Watford at the start of September. Troy Deeney and Craig Cathcart scored for the home side that day. Eventual Premier League runners-up Liverpool ran out 2-1 winners at Wembley a few weeks later, with Erik Lamela getting our consolation goal in the game.

We returned to winning ways with back-to-back triumphs towards the end of the month. A Kane penalty and a Lamela strike saw us to a 2-1 victory at Brighton & Hove Albion while a brace from our number 10 gave us a 2-0 success at Huddersfield Town.

PREMIER LEAGUE REVIEW

NOVEMBER

Lamela scored again in an entertaining 3-2 victory at Wolverhampton Wanderers. We were 3-0 up after 61 minutes, with Lucas and Kane also on target at Molineux. Late penalties from Ruben Neves and Raul Jimenez for the home side made for a nervy finish, but our lads held on to claim all three points.

Our 100% away record continued as Argentine defender Juan Foyth scored his first goal for us in our 1-0 win at Crystal Palace. One of our most impressive performances of the season saw us beat London rivals Chelsea 3-1 at Wembley, goals coming from Dele, Kane and a superb solo effort from Heung-Min Son, as we ended the month in third position in the Premier League table.

DECEMBER

Despite leading 2-1 at the Emirates, we went down to a 4-2 defeat to Arsenal in December. Mauricio Pochettino's men quickly responded from that disappointment with a run of five consecutive League victories.

The first came with a 3-1 triumph over Southampton at Wembley, with Kane, Lucas and Son all scoring. 'Sonny' netted again three days later as we won 2-0 at Leicester City while Dele got our second at the King Power Stadium. A stoppage-time winner from Christian Eriksen saw us beat a spirited Burnley side 1-0 before we produced a classic performance at Goodison Park.

We were three up by half-time on our visit to Everton, thanks to goals from Son, Dele and Kane. Our ruthlessness in front of goal continued in the second period with Son and Kane scoring once again while Eriksen also got in on the act. We made it 11 goals in two matches, as we demolished AFC Bournemouth 5-0 at Wembley a few days later. Son managed another brace while Eriksen, Lucas and Kane were also on target.

Despite leading 1-0 at half-time through a Kane goal, the year ended with a disappointing 3-1 home loss to Wolves.

JANUARY

First-half strikes from Kane, Eriksen and Son saw us win 3-0 at Cardiff City on New Year's Day. After a 1-0 defeat to Manchester United at Wembley, we responded with four straight Premier League victories. Harry Winks's dramatic winner at Fulham, three minutes into added time, completed our comeback at Craven Cottage. We trailed at the break, after Fernando Llorente put through his own net. Dele drew us level before Wink's magical moment!

We left it late to beat Watford too. Son and Llorente's goals that sealed a 2-1 win against the Hornets both came in the last 10 minutes of the game at Wembley, after we trailed at half-time to a Craig Cathcart strike.

FEBRUARY

There were seven minutes of normal time remaining when Son got the only goal of the game at home to Newcastle United, as Pochettino's side continued to serve up late winners. Our 3-1 triumph over Leicester City at Wembley was slightly more comfortable as goals from Davinson Sanchez and Eriksen either side of half-time put us two-up against the Foxes. While Jamie Vardy got one back for the Foxes, Son's stoppage time effort made sure of our win. Hugo Lloris saved a penalty from Vardy when we were leading 1-0.

A 2-1 defeat at Burnley and a 2-0 loss at Chelsea effectively put us out of the race for the Premier League title but our quest for a top four finish and a place in the UEFA Champions League remained on course.

MARCH

Lloris was our penalty king once again, keeping out a stoppage-time spot-kick from Pierre Emerick Aubameyang in the north London derby. After going behind that afternoon, we levelled thanks to a successful penalty from Kane. The match, watched by our largest crowd of the season of 81,332, was our final 'home' fixture at Wembley Stadium.

Late goals cost us dearly as we went down to back-to-back 2-1 defeats at Southampton and Liverpool. Having led at St Mary's through a strike from Kane, James Ward-Prowse's 81st minute free-kick gave Saints maximum points. Lucas drew us level at Anfield with 20 minutes left, but Toby Alderweireld put through his own net in the final minute as we were unlucky not to secure at least a draw at Anfield.

APRIL

There was an emotional homecoming on 3 April 2019, as we played our first home match at our new stadium. Son wrote his name into the history books, scoring our first goal there in a 2-0 win over Crystal Palace. Eriksen was also on target on a night to remember in N17.

After Victor Wanyama put us one-up in our home match with Huddersfield Town 10 days later, Lucas achieved another stadium 'first', with a hat-trick in our 4-0 triumph over the Terriers. A 1-0 defeat at Manchester City towards the end of the month came just days after we'd sealed our progress to the UEFA Champions League semi-final at the Etihad Stadium.

Back-to-back home matches yielded a pair of 1-0 results. A late Eriksen strike saw us to victory over Brighton & Hove Albion but we then lost our first match at our new home to West Ham United.

MAY

A stoppage-time header from Nathan Ake gave AFC Bournemouth a 1-0 victory in our penultimate match of the season at the Vitality Stadium. We ended the campaign with a 2-2 home draw with Everton as Dier and Eriksen got our goals.

CARABAO CUP

Spurs 2-2 Watford
(Spurs win 4-2 on penalties)

With Wembley Stadium unavailable and work on our new stadium continuing, we staged our 'home' tie against Watford in the third round of the Carabao Cup at Stadium MK. Isaac Success put the Hornets ahead inside the opening minute of the second half. On his return to his hometown club, Dele levelled from the penalty spot with eight minutes remaining, while Erik Lamela put us in front moments later. Former Spur Etienne Capoue equalised for Watford with a minute of normal time remaining to force a penalty shootout. Heung-Min Son, Lamela, Fernando Llorente and Dele all scored from the spot while our goalkeeper Paulo Gazzaniga saved from Capoue and Domingos Quina to put us through to the next round.

West Ham United 1-3 Spurs

Son celebrated his 150th appearance for us with a brace in our 3-1 victory at the London Stadium. Following the South Korean's strikes either side of half-time, Lucas Perez got a goal back for the Hammers with 19 minutes left on the clock. Llorente sealed our win with a left-footed volley past West Ham goalkeeper Adrian.

QUARTER FINAL

Arsenal 0-2 Spurs

Son was on target once again as we put on a convincing display to beat rivals Arsenal at the Emirates Stadium. Dele doubled our advantage in the second half, getting on the end of a perfectly weighted long-ball from Harry Kane before chipping Petr Cech.

SEMI FINAL - FIRST LEG

Spurs 1-0 Chelsea

We gained a slender advantage in our two-legged semi-final with Chelsea with a 1-0 victory at Wembley Stadium. We were awarded a 26th minute penalty in the match when Blues keeper Kepa Arrizabalaga fouled Kane in the box. The England striker picked himself up before converting the resulting spot-kick.

SEMI FINAL - SECOND LEG

Chelsea 2-1 Spurs
(Chelsea win 4-2 on penalties)

Chelsea turned the semi-final tie on its head with first-half goals from N'Golo Kante and Eden Hazard at Stamford Bridge. Llorente's second half strike would have carried us through to the final in seasons past on the away goals. With that ruling – along with extra-time – scrapped from the start of the 2018/19 season, the match went to penalties. While Christian Eriksen and Lamela scored, misses from Eric Dier and Lucas Moura proved costly as the Blues won 4-2 on spot-kicks.

FA CUP

THIRD ROUND

Tranmere Rovers 0-7 Spurs

Serge Aurier gave us a first-half lead at League Two side Tranmere Rovers prior to a second-half goal blitz. Fernando Llorente scored a hat-trick after the break while Heung-Min Son also found the back of the net.

Aurier got his second of the night while Harry Kane came off the bench to complete our 7-0 victory. The match saw youngsters George Marsh and Timothy Eyoma make their competitive First Team debuts for us.

FOURTH ROUND

Crystal Palace 2-0 Spurs

Goals from Connor Wickham and ex-Spurs winger Andros Townsend saw us eliminated from the FA Cup after a 2-0 defeat at Selhurst Park.

SPURS WOMEN
ROUND-UP 2018/19

Karen Hills' side made history by gaining promotion to the FA Women's Super League.

Spurs Women made an incredible start to their 2018/19 FA Women's Championship campaign, winning their opening six league fixtures against the likes of London Bees, Leicester City, Crystal Palace, Lewes, Millwall Lionesses and Aston Villa. The Lilywhites' form saw Karen Hills named LMA Manager of the Month for September while striker Rianna Dean was voted FA Women's Championship Player of the Month in October having netted six times in three matches.

Despite heavy defeats at eventual champions Manchester United and at home to Durham, Hills' team remained well and truly in the title race with victories over Charlton Athletic and Crystal Palace towards the end of 2018.

January 2019 yielded three wins out of three against Sheffield United, Lewes and Millwall, while the Lilywhites also had a perfect league record in February with a 3-0 triumph at London Bees and a 1-0 home success against Leicester City. The awards continued to arrive as Hills and Sarah Wiltshire were named the division's manager and player of the month respectively in January.

Manchester United won the FA Women's Championship title on 20 April 2019 with a 7-0 hammering of Crystal Palace. Our 3-2 away win at Charlton Athletic a day later left us within touching distance of the runners-up spot and a coveted place in the FA Women's Super League. This was achieved on 1 May 2019 when our women drew 1-1 at Aston Villa with Jessica Naz on target. The season ended with a 2-0 win at Durham, which saw Anna Filbey bag a second-half brace.

The Lilywhites reached the fifth round of the FA Women's Cup during the 2018/19 season, winning 3-0 at Crystal Palace prior to a 3-0 defeat to eventual competition winners Manchester City in front of a record home crowd of 1,158 at Cheshunt FC's Theobalds Lane ground. Hills' side finished fourth in the Continental Tyres Cup Group One South meanwhile.

At the end of the campaign, the team changed their name from 'Tottenham Hotspur Ladies' to 'Tottenham Hotspur Women' ahead of their inaugural season in the FA Women's Super League.

> Our Academy
> and Development
> squads took part
> in a variety of
> competitions during
> the 2018/19 season

YOUTH TEAM
ROUND-UP 2018/19

Premier League 2

Our Under-23 side finished ninth in the table with seven wins, seven draws and eight defeats. Jack Roles scored eight goals in 19 appearances in the division, including a hat-trick in our 3-1 victory over Derby County at the Lamex Stadium, Stevenage in our final Premier League 2 match of the season.

Under-18 Premier League

Our Under-18 team won 18 of their 22 league fixtures as they came second in their domestic league in 2018/19. Season highlights included a 9-0 victory at West Ham United, a 3-2 home triumph over eventual-champions Arsenal and a 3-1 win against Southampton on 24 March 2019 in the inaugural football match to be played at our new stadium. J'Neil Bennett scored the first-ever goal at the ground in the win.

UEFA Youth League

We competed in the UEFA Youth League for the third consecutive season in 2018/19, finishing second in Group B – behind Barcelona but above Inter and PSV Eindhoven – with two wins, three draws and just one defeat. Goals from Troy Parrott and Rodel Richards gave us a 2-0 win away to Barcelona in our final group fixture to seal our progress to the knock-out phase. We beat Greek side PAOK 1-0 in the play-off round before losing 2-0 to eventual tournament winners Porto in the round of 16.

v Barcelona

v Southampton

v Millwall

v Derby County

v Athletic Bilbao

Checkatrade Trophy

Our Under-21s beat the first team of League One side Gillingham 4-0 during our Checkatrade Trophy campaign. We finished second in the Southern Section Group A of the competition, behind eventual winners Portsmouth, as we drew 1-1 with Crawley Town and lost 3-2 to Pompey. We were beaten 3-0 at Oxford United in round two of the tournament.

Premier League International Cup

Our Under-23 side topped Group F of the Premier League International Cup with a 2-1 win over VfL Wolfsburg, a 2-2 draw with Norwich City and a 5-4 triumph against Athletic Bilbao. We were beaten 1-0 by Croatian side Dinamo Zagreb in the quarter finals, who went on to reach the final before losing 2-0 to Bayern Munich.

Under-18 Premier League Cup

Victories over Wolverhampton Wanderers and Swansea City, as well as a draw with Middlesbrough saw us finish second in Group A of the Under-18 Premier League Cup and progress to the knockout phase as one of the competition's best runners-up. Alas, we were beaten 2-0 by Derby County in the quarter finals.

FA Youth Cup

Substitute J'Neil Bennett scored a late equaliser in our FA Youth Cup third round tie at Millwall to force extra-time at The Den. Progress to the next round was secured when Rodel Richards struck home to give us a 2-1 win. We twice led in our fourth round match against Arsenal, only to lose 5-2 after extra-time at Boreham Wood's Meadow Park stadium.

MAURICIO POCHETTINO

In his fifth season as Spurs manager, 2018/19 proved to be another hugely successful campaign with Mauricio Pochettino at the helm.

The standout achievement was of course our run to the UEFA Champions League Final. We progressed from Group B of the competition, which contained Barcelona, Inter Milan and PSV Eindhoven, to make it through to the knockout phase. Subsequent victories over Borussia Dortmund, Manchester City and Ajax will live long in the memory, as will Mauricio's reaction to those historic triumphs. Lucas Moura's dramatic stoppage time winner at the Johan Cruyff ArenA in our semi-final, second leg match against Ajax brought our manager to his knees and saw him shed tears of joy!

For a third consecutive season, we reached the last four of a domestic cup competition, beating Watford, West Ham United and Arsenal in the Carabao Cup before defeat to Chelsea in a penalty shootout at the end of our semi-final, second leg tie. We had competed in the FA Cup semi-final in the two previous campaigns.

In the Premier League, we achieved a top four finish and qualification to the Champions League for a fourth consecutive season.

There was recognition for Mauricio's achievements during the season, as he was named Manager of the Year at the London Football Awards on the same night Heung-Min Son claimed the Player of the Year gong. The Argentine had previously won three Premier League Manager of the Month awards during his time at Spurs.

Mauricio was born in Murphy in Argentina on 2 March 1972 and won 20 caps for his country, scoring twice, during a distinguished playing career. Having represented Argentine side Newell's Old Boys as a youngster, he moved to Europe in 1994 to join Spanish club Espanyol. He subsequently played for Paris Saint-Germain and Bordeaux before returning to Espanyol in 2004 – first on loan, then on a permanent deal. He hung up his boots two years later.

His managerial career began at Espanyol, before a successful spell at Southampton. In his first full season at St Mary's in 2013/14, he guided Saints to an eighth-place finish in the League – their highest position since 2002/03 and their best points tally of the Premier League era.

In his first season in charge of Spurs in 2014/15, we reached the Football League Cup Final and finished fifth in the Premier League.

Mauricio's Spurs Record
(All competitive, first-team matches up to and including the 2018/19 season)

Matches;
Played: 276
Won: 154
Drawn: 55
Lost: 67
Win percentage: 55.8%

MEET MAURICIO'S COACHING STAFF

Jesús Pérez
Assistant Manager

Born in Spain on 5 October 1971, Jesús has previously worked with Mauricio as a first team analyst at Spanish club Espanyol, while he served as his Assistant Manager at Premier League side Southampton. The UEFA Pro Licence holder has almost two decades' experience of coaching, having also held posts with the likes of Al Ittihad, Almeria, Rayo Vallecano, Pontevedra, Real Murcia, Castellon and Tarragona.

Miguel D'Agostino
First Team Coach

Miguel was a teammate of Mauricio's at Argentine side Newell's Old Boys in the early 1990s. The defender also turned out for the likes of Gimnasia y Esgrima, Ecuadorian side LDU de Quito and Chilean outfit C.D. Palestino during his playing career as well as Spain's SD Compostela and French sides Chamois Niortais, Canet en Rousillon and Angoulême CFC, where he was Player-Coach. He served as Assistant Manager and, later, Chief Scout at Stade Brestois 29 while he also held a role as Assistant Coach at Dubai CSC in the United Arab Emirates. He has since worked under Mauricio at Espanyol, Southampton and Spurs.

Toni Jiménez
Goalkeeping Coach

Toni is a former Spanish international goalkeeper, who played over 350 league matches for the likes of Rayo Vallecano, Atletico Madrid, Elche and Espanyol during his career. He was selected in Spain's squad for the 1992 Olympic Games in his home city of Barcelona, playing all six games as they won the gold medal for men's football. Toni served as Goalkeeping Coach at Espanyol under Mauricio's management between 2009 and 2012 and has since held the same role at Southampton and Spurs.

HUGO LLORIS

The 2019/20 season marks Hugo's eighth season as a Spurs player, having joined us from Olympique Lyonnais in the summer of 2012. He holds our Club record for the most clean sheets of the Premier League era, with 86 shut-outs in the division as of the end of the 2018/19 season. Captain for both club and country, Hugo has played over 100 times for France and lifted the World Cup with them in 2018.

RYAN SESSEGNON

Ryan signed for us from Fulham in August 2019 at the age of 19. After making his senior debut for the Whites aged 16 years and 81 days, he went on to make a total of 120 appearances for the West Londoners, netting 25 times. Able to operate as either a full-back or winger, Ryan has been capped by England at various youth and development levels. He was named in the Team of the Tournament at the 2017 UEFA European Under-19 Championship as the Young Lions won the competition for the first time. He was included in England's squad for the 2019 UEFA European Under-21 Championships.

DANNY ROSE

Danny featured in 37 matches during the 2018/19 season, including eight in the UEFA Champions League. Our longest-serving player ended the campaign just two appearances short of 200 games in our colours, during which time he scored ten goals. The former Leeds United trainee was part of England's squad that finished third at the UEFA Nations League finals in 2019.

TOBY ALDERWEIRELD

Having been plagued by injuries during the 2017/18 season, Toby was a regular feature in our back-line during the 2018/19 campaign with 50 appearances in all competitions. The Belgian international, who had won nearly 100 caps for his country at the time of writing, was one of four former Ajax players to feature in our Champions League semi-final victory over the Dutch side during the season.

JAN VERTONGHEN

The most capped Belgian international of all-time, Jan made 34 appearances for us during the 2018/19 season – his seventh campaign as a Spurs player. The defender scored our first goal of that particular season in a 2-1 win at Newcastle United. He was also on target and made an assist in our 3-0 home win over Borussia Dortmund in the Champions League in February 2019.

DAVINSON SANCHEZ

Along with Toby and Jan, Davinson is another defender who formerly played for Ajax. The Colombian international signed for us from the Dutch club in the summer of 2017 and had played 78 matches for us by the end of 2018/19. He put pen-to-paper on an improved contact after his debut season with the Club, committing his future to us until 2024. His first-ever Spurs goal came in our 3-1 win over Leicester City in February 2019.

SERGE AURIER

Ivory Coast international Serge featured in 17 matches for us in all competitions during the 2018/19 season, including five Champions League games. Having scored twice in 24 appearances in his inaugural campaign in our colours in 2017/18, following a move from Paris Saint-Germain, he matched that tally last season thanks to a brace in our 7-0 win at Tranmere Rovers in the FA Cup in January 2019.

KYLE WALKER-PETERS

Kyle played ten matches in all competitions during the 2018/19 season including starting in our 1-1 draw at Barcelona in the Champions League. On Boxing Day 2018, the defender made three assists in our 5-0 victory over Bournemouth in the Premier League. The England Under-20 World Cup winner made his debut for us away to Newcastle United back in August 2017.

JUAN FOYTH

Having arrived from Estudiantes in the summer of 2017, Juan made 23 appearances in his first two seasons at Spurs. His first goal came in our 1-0 win at Crystal Palace in the Premier League in November 2018. He made his senior debut for Argentina against Mexico in a 2-0 victory that same month.

TANGUY NDOMBELE

A product of EA Guingamp's youth system, Tanguy started his senior professional career with Ligue 2 outfit Amiens before moving to Olympique Lyonnais, firstly on loan in August 2017 then on a permanent deal in the summer of 2018. He made 96 appearances for Lyon, scoring four goals and making 16 assists before signing for us in July 2019. Tanguy was included in the 2018/19 Ligue 1 Team of the Year alongside the likes of Neymar and Kylian Mbappe. He made his senior international debut for France against Iceland in October 2018.